First World War
and Army of Occupation
War Diary
France, Belgium and Germany

59 DIVISION
177 Infantry Brigade
Leicestershire Regiment
2/4th Battalion.
27 October 1915 - 14 February 1916

WO95/3022/3

The Naval & Military Press Ltd
www.nmarchive.com
Published in association with The National Archives

Published by

The Naval & Military Press Ltd

Unit 10 Ridgewood Industrial Park,

Uckfield, East Sussex,

TN22 5QE England

Tel: +44 (0) 1825 749494

www.naval-military-press.com

www.nmarchive.com

This diary has been reprinted in facsimile from the original. Any imperfections are inevitably reproduced and the quality may fall short of modern type and cartographic standards.

© Crown Copyright
Images reproduced by permission of The National Archives, London, England, 2015.

Contents

Document type	Place/Title	Date From	Date To
Heading	WO95/3022/3 1916 Jan-Feb 2/4 Battalion Leicestershire Regiment		
War Diary	War Diary Of 2/4 Leicestershire Regiment From January 1st 1916 To January 31st 1916		
War Diary	Harpenden	27/10/1915	07/01/1916
War Diary	Luton	19/01/1916	14/02/1916
Heading	War Diary Of 2/4th Bn. Leicestershire Regt. For Month of February 1916		

WO/95/3022/3

1916 Jan-Feb

2/4 Battalion Leicestershire Regiment

Confidential
War Diary
of
2/4 Leicestershire Regiment

From Jany 1st 1916 to Jany 31st 1916.

C. F. Oliver Lieut Col
2/4 Leicestershire Regt

WAR DIARY 2/4 LEICESTER REGT
INTELLIGENCE SUMMARY

Army Form C. 2118.

(Erase heading not required.)

Hour, Date, Place	Summary of Events and Information	Remarks and references to Appendices
27.10.15 HARPENDEN	2/Lt. H.R. POCHIN, L.F.H.W. de SZARKOWICZ, B.T.C. GILBERT, joined and L.G. BARTON, left for B.E.F.	
26.10.15 "	draft of 16 men joined from 3/4 Bn.	
18.10.15 "	2/Lt. U.S.F. LEAHARD left for B.E.F.	
14.11.15 "	MAJOR GENERAL R.H.R. REHOE C.B. took over Division commanded by G.O.C.	Previous
17.11.15 "	Inspection by G.O.C. withdrawn + 1,303 after review	
22.11.15 "	Interview after	
	BRIGADIER GENERAL C.G. BLACKADER D.S.O took over command of Brigade vice Col. G.H. JACKSON T.D	
7.1.16 "	" " " " " killed in LUTON	
19.1.16 LUTON	Battalion moved to billets in LUTON	
22.1.16 "	39 Scots recruits joined	
24.1.16 "	48 " "	
25.1.16 "	46 " "	
26.1.16 "	2/Lt. R.F. WAGSTAFFE transferred to 3/4 here Regl	
27.1.16 "	150 men about M.L.E. rifles sent to Units	

Army Form C. 2118.

WAR DIARY
or
INTELLIGENCE SUMMARY. 2/4 LEICESTER REGT.
(Erase heading not required.)

Instructions regarding War Diaries and Intelligence Summaries are contained in F. S. Regs., Part II. and the Staff Manual respectively. Title pages will be prepared in manuscript.

Hour, Date, Place	Summary of Events and Information	Remarks and references to Appendices
26.1.16 LUTON	60 "Scot" Recruits joined	803
29.1.16 "	49 " " "	803
14.2.16 "	Major General A.E.SANDBACH.C.B.D.S.O Took over command of the Division from Major General R.N.R.READE.C.B	803

J.F. Buicher Major Lt
Comdt 2/4 Leic Regt

Confidential

War Diary

of

2/4th Bn: Leicestershire Regt.

for Month of February 1916

E. T. Oliver.
Lieut: Colonel
Commanding 2/4th Leicestershire Regt.

www.ingramcontent.com/pod-product-compliance
Lightning Source LLC
Chambersburg PA
CBHW081516160426
43193CB00014B/2705